STATE PROFILES
DELAWARE

BY COLLEEN SEXTON

BELLWETHER MEDIA • MINNEAPOLIS, MN

Blastoff! Discovery launches a new mission: reading to learn. Filled with facts and features, each book offers you an exciting new world to explore!

BLASTOFF! UNIVERSE

BLASTOFF! Beginners — GRADE K

BLASTOFF! READERS — GRADES 1-3

DISCOVERY — GRADE 4

This edition first published in 2022 by Bellwether Media, Inc.

No part of this publication may be reproduced in whole or in part without written permission of the publisher.
For information regarding permission, write to Bellwether Media, Inc., Attention: Permissions Department,
6012 Blue Circle Drive, Minnetonka, MN 55343.

Library of Congress Cataloging-in-Publication Data

Names: Sexton, Colleen A., 1967- author.
Title: Delaware / by Colleen Sexton.
Description: Minneapolis, MN : Bellwether Media, Inc., 2022. | Series: Blastoff! Discovery: State Profiles | Includes bibliographical references and index. | Audience: Ages 7-13 | Audience: Grades 4-6 | Summary: "Engaging images accompany information about Delaware. The combination of high-interest subject matter and narrative text is intended for students in grades 3 through 8"– Provided by publisher.
Identifiers: LCCN 2021019693 (print) | LCCN 2021019694 (ebook) | ISBN 9781644873793 (library binding) | ISBN 9781648341564 (ebook)
Subjects: LCSH: Delaware–Juvenile literature.
Classification: LCC F164.3 .S48 2022 (print) | LCC F164.3 (ebook) | DDC 975.1–dc23
LC record available at https://lccn.loc.gov/2021019693
LC ebook record available at https://lccn.loc.gov/2021019694

Editor: Rebecca Sabelko   Designer: Kathleen Petelinsek

Printed in the United States of America, North Mankato, MN.

TABLE OF CONTENTS

BEACH BUILDING

Beachgoers of all ages enter Rehoboth Beach's Sandcastle Contest each September. Crowds watch teams build castles, mermaids, dolphins, and other creations out of sand.

It is a hot summer day in Delaware. A family arrives in the Atlantic coastal town of Rehoboth Beach. The smell of popcorn and saltwater taffy fills the air as they stroll down the town's famous boardwalk. The family stops at Funland amusement park to ride the bumper cars and play arcade games.

AIR MOBILITY COMMAND MUSEUM

CAPE HENLOPEN STATE PARK

DOVER INTERNATIONAL SPEEDWAY

NEMOURS MANSION AND GARDENS

REHOBOTH BEACH

Soon, it is time to hit the beach! The family spreads out their towels on the sand. They jump into the cool ocean waves and spend the afternoon swimming. The family ends their day at the beach with ice cream cones. Welcome to Delaware!

Delaware sits in the **mid-Atlantic** region. With an area of 2,489 square miles (6,446 square kilometers), it is the second-smallest state. Delaware lies mostly on the Delmarva **Peninsula**. It shares this stretch of land with Maryland and Virginia.

Maryland wraps around Delaware in the south and west. Delaware has a short northern border with Pennsylvania. New Jersey lies to the east across the Delaware River and Delaware Bay. The Atlantic Ocean meets the state's southeastern shore. The capital, Dover, sits in the center of the state. Wilmington, in the north, is the state's largest city.

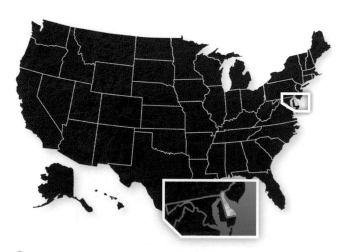

PENNSYLVANIA

MARYLAND

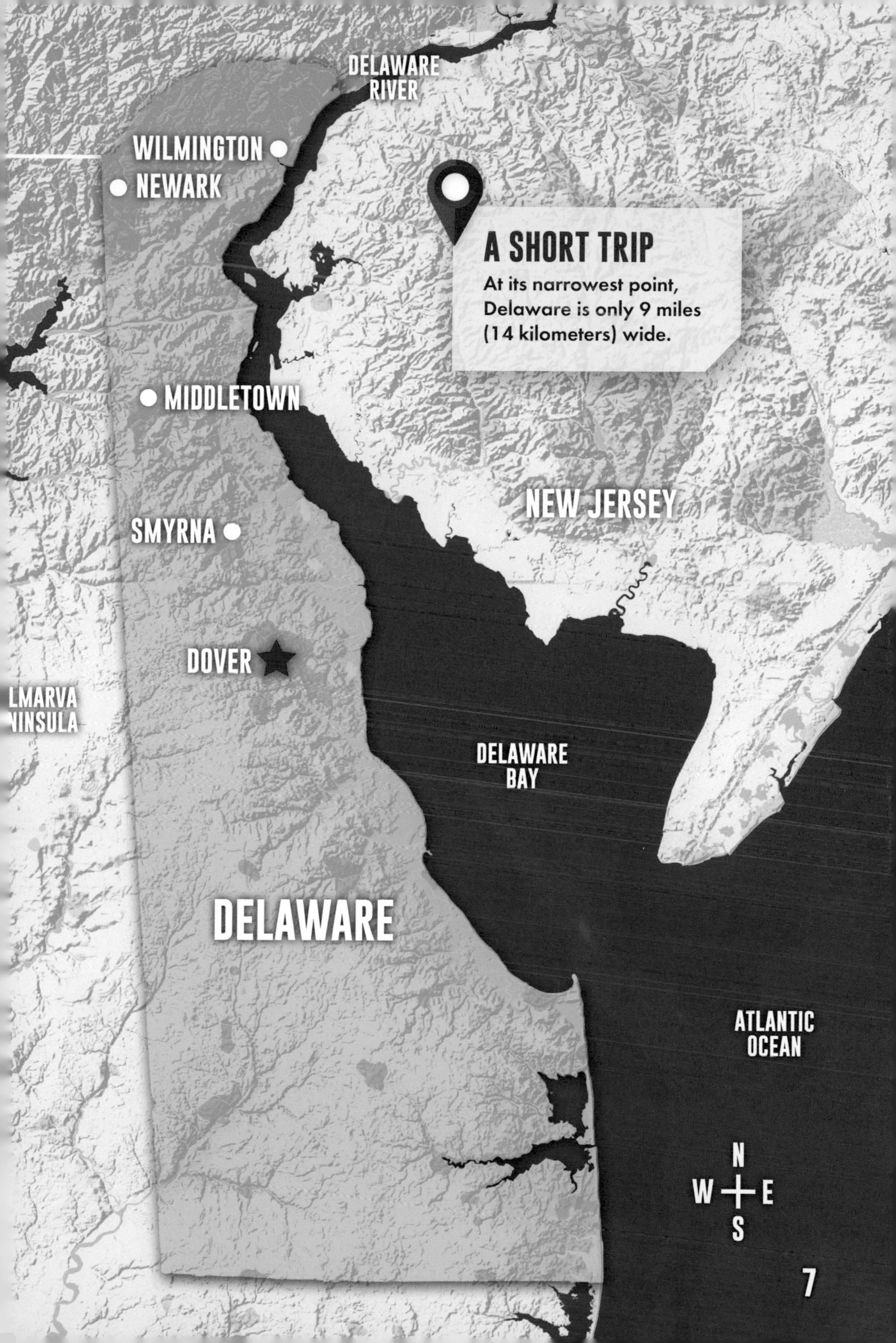

DELAWARE RIVER

WILMINGTON
NEWARK

MIDDLETOWN

SMYRNA

DOVER

LMARVA
NINSULA

DELAWARE

A SHORT TRIP
At its narrowest point, Delaware is only 9 miles (14 kilometers) wide.

NEW JERSEY

DELAWARE BAY

ATLANTIC OCEAN

N
W E
S

HENRY HUDSON WITH
NATIVE AMERICANS

People first arrived in Delaware around 12,000 years ago. Over time, two Native American groups formed. The Lenape Indians lived along the Delaware River in the north. The Nanticoke Indians lived in the south. Both groups built villages and farmed the land. In 1609, English explorer Henry Hudson sailed up Delaware Bay. Dutch and Swedish **settlers** soon followed. More Europeans arrived, pushing the Lenape and Nanticoke westward.

In 1664, England took control of the region. Delaware became 1 of the 13 English **colonies**. The colonies fought the **Revolutionary War** for their independence. In 1787, Delaware became the first state to approve the U.S. **Constitution**.

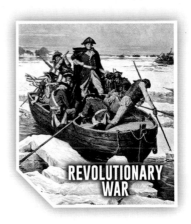

REVOLUTIONARY WAR

NATIVE PEOPLES OF DELAWARE

LENAPE INDIANS

- Original lands around the Delaware River in Delaware, Pennsylvania, New Jersey, and New York

- More than 600 in Delaware today

- Also called Lenni Lenape and Delaware

NANTICOKE INDIAN TRIBE

- Original lands in southwestern Delaware and eastern Maryland

- Around 1,000 in Delaware today

LENAPE HOUSE

Delaware's highest land is in the Piedmont. This region in the state's northern tip features rolling hills and valleys. The wide Delaware River flows south to Delaware Bay. The rest of Delaware lies in the Atlantic Coastal **Plain**. Woodlands and fields cover this low, flat land. Marshes line Delaware's shore. Farther south, **dunes** and sandy beaches stretch along the short Atlantic coast. The Great Cypress Swamp in the south is the state's largest wetland.

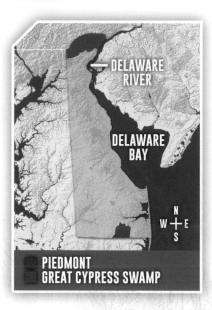

DELAWARE RIVER

DELAWARE BAY

N W E S

PIEDMONT
GREAT CYPRESS SWAMP

DELAWARE'S FUTURE: RISING SEA LEVELS

An increase in global temperatures is causing ice to melt in polar regions. Sea levels are rising. In Delaware, the coastal marshlands will not be able to soak up the added water. Inland areas will flood as a result.

GREAT CYPRESS SWAMP

SPRING
HIGH: 62°F (17°C)
LOW: 42°F (6°C)

SUMMER
HIGH: 84°F (29°C)
LOW: 65°F (18°C)

FALL
HIGH: 66°F (19°C)
LOW: 47°F (8°C)

WINTER
HIGH: 42°F (6°C)
LOW: 26°F (-3°C)

°F = degrees Fahrenheit
°C = degrees Celsius

DELAWARE RIVER

Delaware has hot, **humid** summers. Winters are mild and snowy. Residents stay prepared for any kind of weather. Blizzards, tornadoes, and **hurricanes** can all strike the state.

Delaware's fields and forests shelter a wide variety of animals. Gray foxes hunt mice and rabbits. Deer munch on grasses and leaves. Muskrats and snapping turtles make homes in marshes. Bass, carp, and white perch swim in rivers and lakes. The state's coastal waters are home to crabs, clams, oysters, and sea trout.

Delaware's beaches and marshes attract many birds. Egrets and herons wade in shallow waters. Ospreys, eagles, and hawks soar across the sky in search of prey. Each year, thousands of birds travel through Delaware. Spring brings plovers, sandpipers, and other shorebirds that nest on beaches.

EASTERN SNAPPING TURTLE

WHITE-TAILED DEER

ATLANTIC HORSESHOE CRAB

SNOWY EGRET

BLACK-CROWNED NIGHT HERON

GRAY FOX

Life Span: up to 10 years
Status: least concern

gray fox range = ■

LEAST CONCERN	NEAR THREATENED	VULNERABLE	ENDANGERED	CRITICALLY ENDANGERED	EXTINCT IN THE WILD	EXTINCT
▲						

13

Around 990,000 people live in Delaware. Two out of every three Delawareans live in and around Wilmington. The south is more **rural**. Farms and small towns lie outside Dover. Delaware's coastal communities in the southeast draw many retired people.

LEWES

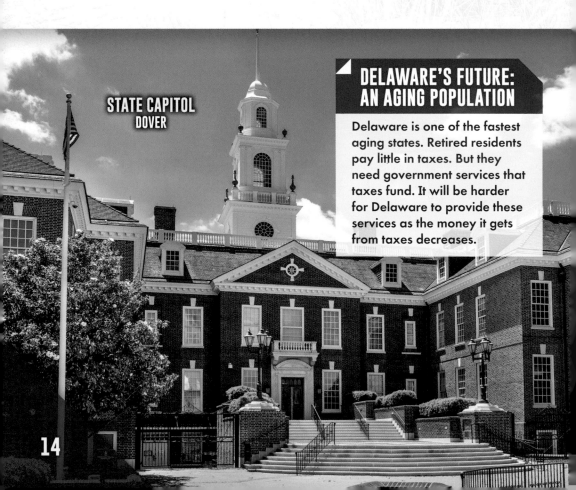

STATE CAPITOL
DOVER

DELAWARE'S FUTURE: AN AGING POPULATION

Delaware is one of the fastest aging states. Retired residents pay little in taxes. But they need government services that taxes fund. It will be harder for Delaware to provide these services as the money it gets from taxes decreases.

FAMOUS DELAWAREAN

Name: Joseph R. Biden
Born: November 20, 1942
Hometown: Wilmington, Delaware
Famous For: Delaware senator for 35 years who served as vice president from 2009 to 2017 and became the 46th president of the United States in 2021

In the 1800s, many of Delaware's early **immigrants** were from Ireland, Germany, Italy, Poland, and Russia. Today, Delaware's population includes **descendants** of these immigrants. More recent arrivals come from Mexico, India, China, Guatemala, and Jamaica. About one in five Delawareans is African American or Black. Small numbers of Lenape and Nanticoke Indians live in the state.

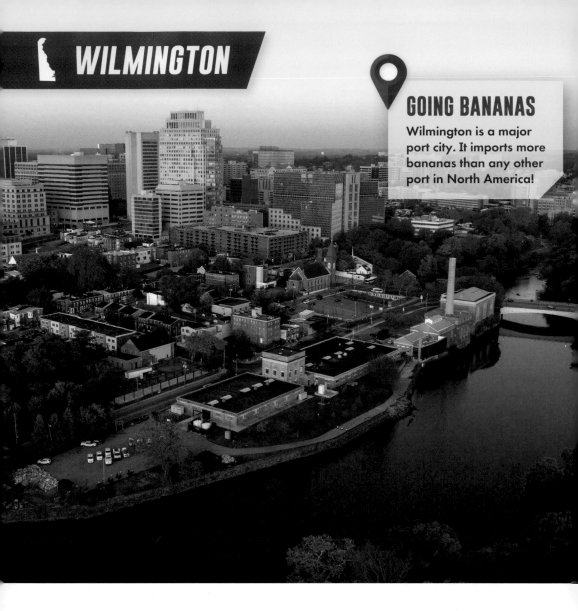

WILMINGTON

GOING BANANAS

Wilmington is a major port city. It imports more bananas than any other port in North America!

In 1638, Swedish settlers built Fort Christina. It was Delaware's first permanent European settlement. Fort Christina rose where Brandywine Creek and the Christina River meet the Delaware River. The settlement grew and became Wilmington in 1739. Today, Wilmington is the state's largest city. It is also part of a **metropolitan** area that includes Philadelphia, Pennsylvania, and Camden, New Jersey.

Wilmington's historic buildings mix with modern high-rises. Locals stroll the Riverwalk and enjoy the Riverfront's many shops and restaurants. Artwork at the Delaware Art Museum and live theater performances at The Grand draw many audiences. Brandywine Park is one of many popular parks.

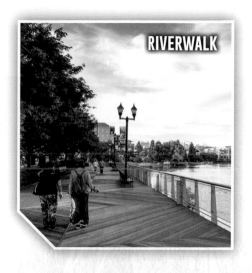

RIVERWALK

BRANDYWINE PARK

Delaware's early settlers were farmers and fishers. Today, many farmers raise chickens. They also grow corn, soybeans, and other vegetables. Fishing crews haul in crabs, oysters, and clams. Northern Delaware is a center of industry. Several large chemical companies employ many Delawareans. They make medicines, dyes, rubber, and nylon.

Most working Delawareans have **service jobs**. Finance is an important service industry. Large banks offer credit cards and help customers manage their money. **Tourism** offers service workers summer jobs in resorts along the coast.

A CHEMICAL GIANT

Wilmington is the headquarters for DuPont. The company was founded as a gunpowder mill in 1802. It grew into one of the biggest chemical companies in the world!

INVENTED IN DELAWARE

NYLON
Date Invented: 1935
Inventor: Wallace Carothers
(DuPont)

KEVLAR
Date Invented: 1965
Inventor: Stephanie Kwolek
(DuPont)

A TOP CROP

Delaware's largest fruit crop is watermelons. Cooks grill the fruit and make it into soups and salads.

Seafood tops the list of favorite foods in Delaware. Blue crabs pulled from Delaware Bay are steamed or made into crab cakes. Cooks serve up a **traditional** fish stew called muddle. Chicken with biscuits or vegetables is a popular dish. Delawareans also enjoy slippery dumplings. Cooks roll dough thinly and cut it into squares. Then, they boil the squares in chicken broth.

Saltwater taffy, ice cream, and french fries with vinegar are favorites on Delaware's boardwalks. Bakers use Delaware-grown peaches in peach pie, the state's official dessert. Apple **orchards** produce the apple cider used to fry up apple cider donuts.

MUDDLE

SALTWATER TAFFY

35 TO 40 PIECES

Have an adult help you make this recipe.

INGREDIENTS

1 1/4 cups white sugar

4 teaspoons cornstarch

1/2 cup light corn syrup

1/2 cup water

1 tablespoon butter, plus more for greasing

1/2 teaspoon sea salt

2 teaspoons flavored extract of choice

1/4 teaspoon vanilla extract

food coloring

DIRECTIONS

1. Grease a baking sheet with butter. Set aside.

2. In a saucepan, combine the sugar and cornstarch. Add the corn syrup, water, butter, and salt. Stir over medium heat until the butter melts and the mixture comes to a boil.

3. Cook without stirring until the mixture reaches 250 degrees Fahrenheit (121 degrees Celsius). Remove from heat, and stir in the flavored extract and food coloring.

4. Pour the mixture onto the cookie sheet, and let it cool for about 15 minutes.

5. Grease your hands, and pull and stretch the taffy until it lightens in color and stiffens.

6. Form into ropes, cut into pieces with buttered scissors, and wrap the pieces in wax paper. Enjoy for a sweet treat!

THE MONSTER MILE

The Dover International Speedway is also known as the Monster Mile. A monster statue holding a race car guards the track's entrance!

Delaware's sports fans root for the Wilmington Blue Rocks baseball and Delaware Blue Coats basketball teams. Crowds also cheer on the University of Delaware's sports teams. NASCAR racing thrills fans at Dover International Speedway. Delaware's sunny beaches draw sailors, surfers, and kite-flyers. Swimmers and boaters flock to rivers and lakes. Campers enjoy starry nights in state parks.

Winterthur Museum is one of the state's many museums. Its Enchanted Woods invite children to follow a maze to a fairy cottage. Visitors to New Castle walk the town's historic cobblestone streets. Some buildings date to the late 1600s!

WINTERTHUR MUSEUM ENCHANTED WOODS

NOTABLE SPORTS TEAM

Wilmington Blue Rocks
Sport: High-A Minor League Baseball
Started: 1993
Place of Play: Frawley Stadium

FESTIVALS AND TRADITIONS

DOVER DAYS

Every May, Delawareans celebrate their **heritage** at Dover Days. Highlights include **maypole** dancing and hot air balloon rides. In June, the African American Festival features a drum and dance parade. The Delaware State Fair draws big crowds every July. Grandstand events include a rodeo and a demolition derby.

DELAWARE STATE FAIR

Rehoboth Beach hosts the Sea Witch Halloween and Fiddler's Festival in October. Fun events include a dog costume parade, a cackle contest, and a broom-tossing contest. Banjo and fiddle players also entertain the crowd. Delaware's festivals show off the state's fun-loving spirit!

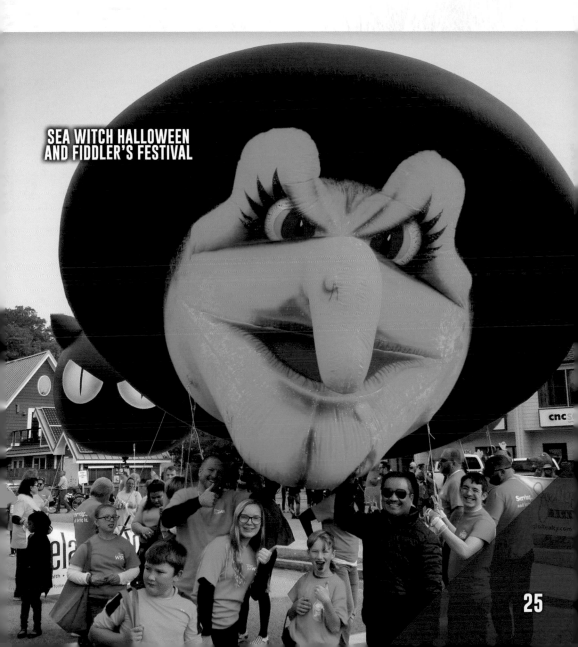

SEA WITCH HALLOWEEN AND FIDDLER'S FESTIVAL

DELAWARE TIMELINE

1609

English explorer Henry Hudson enters Delaware Bay

1829

The Chesapeake and Delaware Canal opens, connecting the Delaware River to Chesapeake Bay

1787

Delaware becomes the first U.S. state

1664

England takes control of the Delaware colony

1800

Wilmington becomes the last stop on the Underground Railroad for some enslaved people seeking freedom in the north

1951

The Delaware Memorial Bridge opens near Wilmington, allowing cars to cross the Delaware River to New Jersey

2000

Ruth Ann Minner is elected Delaware's first female governor

1993

James H. Sills Jr. becomes the first African American mayor of Wilmington

1901

More than 35 years after the Civil War ended, Delaware approves the Thirteenth Amendment, outlawing slavery

2021

Joseph R. Biden of Wilmington is sworn in as the 46th president of the United States

Nicknames: The First State, The Diamond State

State Motto: Liberty and Independence

Date of Statehood: December 7, 1787 (the first state)

Capital City: Dover ★

Other Major Cities: Wilmington, Newark, Middletown, Smyrna

Area: 2,489 square miles (6,446 square kilometers); Delaware is the 49th largest state.

Population

989,948
(2020)

STATE FLAG

LIBERTY AND INDEPENDENCE

DECEMBER 7, 1787

Delaware's state flag has a blue background. It features the state seal inside a tan diamond shape. A farmer and a soldier appear on the state seal. Between them are a ship, an ear of corn, a bundle of wheat, and an ox. They stand for the state's economy. A banner with the state motto is at the bottom of the seal. The date that Delaware became a state lies below the state seal.

INDUSTRY

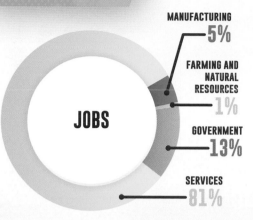

JOBS

MANUFACTURING
5%

FARMING AND NATURAL RESOURCES
1%

GOVERNMENT
13%

SERVICES
81%

Main Exports

medicines

cars

chemistry instruments

bananas

Natural Resources
sand, gravel, magnesium

GOVERNMENT

3 ELECTORAL VOTES

Federal Government

1 REPRESENTATIVE | **2** SENATORS

USA

DE

State Government

41 REPRESENTATIVES | **21** SENATORS

STATE SYMBOLS

STATE BIRD
BLUE HEN CHICKEN

STATE BUTTERFLY
TIGER SWALLOWTAIL

STATE FLOWER
PEACH BLOSSOM

STATE TREE
AMERICAN HOLLY

colonies—distant territories which are under the control of another nation

constitution—the basic laws and principles of a nation

descendants—people related to a person or group of people who lived at an earlier time

dunes—hills of sand

heritage—the traditions, achievements, and beliefs that are part of the history of a group of people

humid—having a lot of moisture in the air

hurricanes—storms formed in the tropics that have violent winds and often have rain and lightning

immigrants—people who move to a new country

maypole—a tall pole decorated with ribbons and flowers

metropolitan—a combined city and suburban area

mid-Atlantic—a region of the United States that includes Delaware, Maryland, Washington, D.C., Pennsylvania, and Virginia, as well as parts of New Jersey, New York, and North Carolina

orchards—areas where fruit or nut trees are grown

peninsula—a section of land that extends out from a larger piece of land and is almost completely surrounded by water

plain—a large area of flat land

Revolutionary War—the war from 1775 to 1783 in which the United States fought for independence from Great Britain

rural—related to the countryside

service jobs—jobs that perform tasks for people or businesses

settlers—people who move to live in a new, undeveloped region

tourism—the business of people traveling to visit other places

traditional—related to customs, ideas, or beliefs handed down from one generation to the next

AT THE LIBRARY

McManus, Lori. *Exploring the Delaware Colony.* North Mankato, Minn.: Capstone Press, 2017.

Miller, Derek. *Delaware.* New York, N.Y.: Cavendish Square, 2020.

Stanley, Joseph. *Delaware (Lenape).* New York, N.Y.: Powerkids Press, 2016.

ON THE WEB

FACTSURFER

Factsurfer.com gives you a safe, fun way to find more information.

1. Go to www.factsurfer.com.

2. Enter "Delaware" into the search box and click 🔍.

3. Select your book cover to see a list of related content.

INDEX

The images in this book are reproduced through the courtesy of: mauritius images GmbH/ Alamy, front cover, pp. 2-3; manfredxy, p. 3 (peach blossoms); Lauren Huddleston, pp. 4-5 (Rehoboth Beach); Jon Arnold Images Ltd/ Alamy, p. 5 (Air Mobility Command Museum); BlueSky2U, p. 5 (Cape Henlopen State Park); Grindstone Media Group, p. 5 (Dover International Speedway); Hemis/ Alamy, p. 5 (Nemours Mansion and Gardens); North Wind Picture Archives/ Alamy, pp. 8 (Henry Hudson with Native Americans), 26 (1609); AF Fotografie/ Alamy, p. 9 (Revolutionary War); Norman Wharton/ Alamy, p. 9 (Lenape House); Wikipedia, pp. 10 (Great Cypress swamp), 15 (Joe Biden), 23 (Winterthur Museum Enchanted Woods), 27 (2000, 2021); Thomas Gari, p. 11 (Delaware River); Yvonne Navalaney, p. 11 (inset); Tathoms, p. 12 (snowy egret); Vicki Bever/ Alamy, p. 12 (eastern snapping turtle); Paul Tessier, p. 12 (white-tailed deer); Weblogiq, p. 12 (Atlantic horseshoe crab); Ondrej Prosicky, p. 12 (black-crowned night heron); Geoffrey Kuchera, p. 13 (gray fox); Khairil Azhar Junos, pp. 14 (Lewes), 17 (Brandywine Park), 25 (Sea Witch Halloween and Fiddler's Festival); Ian Dagnall/ Alamy, p. 14 (state capitol); UPI/ Alamy, p. 15 (Biden background); Real Window Creative, p. 16; Jon Lovette/ Alamy, p. 17 (riverwalk); Design Pics Inc/ Alamy, p. 18; Kristoffer Tripplaar/ Alamy, p. 19 (DuPont background); Helen Sessions/ Alamy, p. 19 (nylon); Nadezda Murmakova, p. 19 (Kevlar); JeniFoto, p. 20 (watermelon salad); Fanfo, p. 21 (muddle); P Maxwell Photography, p. 21 (background taffy); Andre Jenny/ Alamy, p. 22 (The Monster Mile); ZUMA Press/ Alamy, p. 23 (Wilmington Blue Rocks); Luis Carlos Torres, p. 23 (baseball); Dan Laughman/ Flickr, p. 24 (Dover Days); Herb Quick/ Alamy, p. 24 (Delaware State Fair); Harry Collins Photography, pp. 26-27, 28-29, 30-31, 32; Jon Bilous, p. 26 (1829); Mihai_Andritoiu, p. 27 (1951); Uranium, p. 28 (flag); Edwin Remsberg/ Alamy, p. 29 (blue hen chicken); shekure, p. 29 (tiger swallowtail); FabrikaSimf, p. 29 (peach blossom); damann, p. 29 (American holly); Boonchuay1970, p. 31 (watermelon).